10 MINUTE SATs TESTS MATHS

**AGES 5–6
YEAR 1**

KS1

T0326178

Scholastic Education, an imprint of Scholastic Ltd

Book End, Range Road, Witney, Oxfordshire, OX29 0YD

Registered office: Westfield Road, Southam, Warwickshire CV47 0RA

www.scholastic.co.uk

1 2 3 4 5 6 7 8 9   8 9 0 1 2 3 4 5 6 7

British Library Cataloguing-in-Publication Data

A catalogue record for this book is available from the British Library.

ISBN 978-1407-17523-2

Printed and bound by Bell and Bain Ltd, Glasgow

Author
Paul Hollin

Editorial
Rachel Morgan, Audrey Stokes, Kate Baxter, Sarah Chappelow

Cover and Series Design
Scholastic Design Team: Nicolle Thomas and Neil Salt

Design
Scholastic Design Team: Alice Duggan

Cover Illustration
Adam Linley @ Beehive Illustration
Visual Generation @ Shutterstock

Illustrations
Technical Artwork: Dave Morris
Figures: Carys Evans
Banknotes: © Bank of England [2015]

Contents

How to use this book

This book contains nine different sets of maths tests for Year 1, each containing SATs-style questions. Each set comprises an arithmetic test followed by a reasoning test. As a whole, the tests provide full coverage of the test framework for this age group, across the following strands of the maths curriculum: Number; Calculations; Fractions; Measurement; Geometry.

Some questions require a selected response, for example, where children choose the correct answer from several options. Other questions require a constructed response, where children work out and write down their own answer.

A mark scheme, skills check and progress chart are also included towards the end of this book.

Completing the tests

● It is intended that children will take around ten minutes to complete each set of two tests; however, timings at this age are not strict, so allow your child as much time as they need. You may need to read the questions to your child, as they work through the tests, helping them with any tricky vocabulary.

● After your child has completed each set, mark the tests and together identify and practise any areas where your child is less confident. Ask them to complete the next set at a later date, when you feel they have had enough time to practise and improve.

Marks

1. $2 + 5 = \boxed{}$

1

2. $4 - 4 = \boxed{}$

1

3. $10 + 10 + 10 = \boxed{}$

1

10 MINS

4. $13 - 8 = \boxed{}$

1

5. $\boxed{} + 5 = 19$

1

6. $10 + 15 = \boxed{}$

1

Marks

1. Circle the correct words.

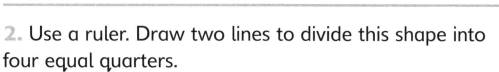

is equal to

18   is less than   15

is more than

1

2. Use a ruler. Draw two lines to divide this shape into four equal quarters.

1

Marks

3. Choose the correct words for each sentence.

above	below	left
right	top	middle
bottom	up	down

a. The boat is at the _____.

1

b. The ball is _____ the teddy.

1

10 MINS

Marks

4. Josh puts 8 black counters on a tray.

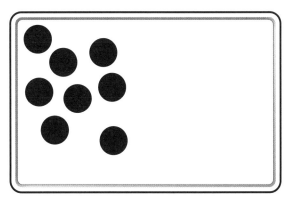

Tina then puts 5 white counters on the tray. How many counters will there be altogether?

counters

1

5. How much money is in this purse?

p

1

Well done! END OF SET A!

SET B
Test 1: Arithmetic

10 MINS

1. 6 + 0 =

1

2. 7 + 8 =

1

3. 20 − 10 =

1

10 MINS

4. $58 - 1 =$ ☐

Marks

1

5. $16 -$ ☐ $= 13$

1

6. $10 + 10 + 10 + 1 =$ ☐

1

1. There are 10 crayons in a box. How many crayons are there in 4 boxes?

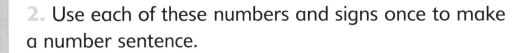

	crayons

Marks

1

2. Use each of these numbers and signs once to make a number sentence.

7	=	6	+	13

1

 KEEP IT GOING!

Marks

3. Three of these shapes are shown in the picture.

Tick them.

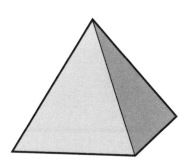 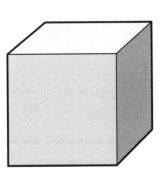 

| cube | cone | pyramid | sphere |

1

4. Mia has a pen, a pencil and an eraser.

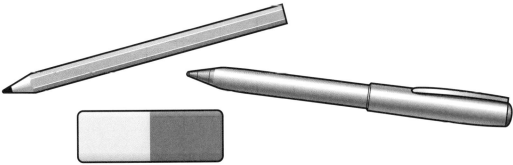

Use a ruler to measure each object. Then complete the sentence:

The _____ is the longest object.

1

10 MINS

5. Tina says:

> Every car has 4 wheels.
> If 5 cars went past my house,
> how many wheels were there?

Marks

 Show your working

wheels

2

6. David has 16 marbles.
He gives away 5.
How many marbles are left?

marbles

1

Well done! END OF SET B!

Marks

1. $7 - 3 =$ ☐

1

2. $7 + 6 =$ ☐

1

3. $14 - 12 =$ ☐

1

10 MINS

4. $4 + 14 = \boxed{}$

Marks

1

5. $103 - 4 = \boxed{}$

1

6. $\boxed{} - 18 = 1$

1

Marks

1. Fill in the missing numbers to make each pair of cards total 9. One has been done for you.

| 8 | 1 |

| | 5 |

| 2 | |

| | 6 |

1

2. Look at the picture.

5 cups of water fill the jug.

4 jugs of water fill the bucket.

How many cups of water will it take to fill the bucket?

 Show your working

| cups |

2

17

3. This is the time.

Draw clock hands to show what time it will be in 4 hours.

Marks

1

KEEP IT GOING!

Marks

4. The numbers below go up by one each time.
Write the missing numbers in words.

six, seven, _____, _____, ten

1

5. The arrow always starts at A.

Fill in the gaps. One has been done for you.

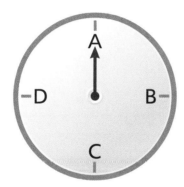

If the arrow is turned a quarter turn clockwise it will
point at ___B___.

If the arrow is turned a half turn clockwise it will
point at _____.

If the arrow is turned a whole turn clockwise it will
point at _____.

If the arrow is turned a three-quarter turn anti-clockwise
it will point at _____.

1

Well done! END OF SET C!

19

SET D
Test 1: Arithmetic

10 MINS

1. $7 + 2 = \boxed{}$

1

2. $8 - 3 = \boxed{}$

1

3. $2 + 2 + 2 + 2 + 2 = \boxed{}$

1

10 MINS

4. $13 - 6 = $ ☐

1

5. $10 + 12 = $ ☐

1

6. ☐ $- 12 = 6$

1

1.

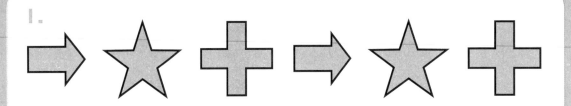

Jill writes the rule for a repeating pattern:

arrow   star   cross

Write the rule for this repeating pattern:

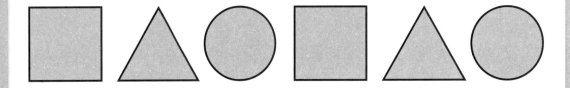

_____

Marks

◯ 1

_____

2. One of these number bonds is wrong. Circle it.

$$4 + 13 = 17 \qquad 12 + 6 = 18$$

$$9 + 7 = 15 \qquad 11 + 5 = 16$$

◯ 1

Marks

3. Gemma has a piece of clay.

If she measures it with a ruler and then cuts it exactly in half, how long will each half be?

cm

1

4. Tim has 14 strawberries. He eats half of them.

How many are left?

strawberries

1

KEEP IT GOING!

10 MINS

Marks

5. There are 16 birds in a tree.

3 more birds arrive, and then 8 fly away.

How many birds are left in the tree?

 Show your working

birds

2

  KEEP IT GOING!

6. A farmer keeps his chickens in groups of 5, and his sheep in pairs.

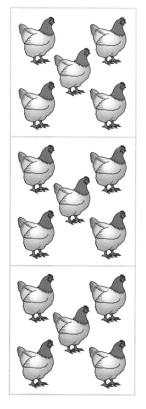

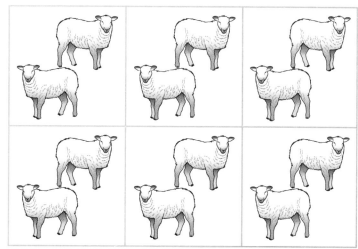

Does he have more or fewer sheep than chickens? Write a **number** and a **word** to complete this sentence.

There are ☐ _____ sheep than chickens.

1

Well done! END OF SET D!

Marks

1. $7 - \boxed{} = 5$

1

2. $6 + 5 = \boxed{}$

1

3. $5 + 5 + 5 = \boxed{}$

1

10 MINS

Marks

4. $15 - 6 =$ ☐

1

5. $3 + 17 =$ ☐

1

6. $19 - 14 =$ ☐

1

10 MINS

Marks

1. George is 117cm tall. Henaz is 1cm more.

How tall is Henaz?

cm

1

2. Kim starts at 96 and counts on 7. Which number will she stop at?

96...

1

10 MINS

3. Class 1 have been weighing fruit.

Marks

pear
40g

orange
60g

apple
50g

banana
30g

a. Complete these sentences. There is more than one possible answer for each sentence.

The _____ is heavier than the

_____.

The _____ is lighter than the

_____.

1

b. Tina puts two pieces of fruit on to a weighing scale. The reading says 100g.

Which **two** pieces of fruit did she choose?

1. _____

KEEP IT GOING!

2. _____

1

10 MINS

Marks

4. A shop is having a sale.

Football stickers

10p

Fun figures

20p

Bouncing balls

30p

If Gina buys 2 bouncing balls, 1 fun figure and 1 football sticker, how much will she spend altogether?

 Show your working

p

2

Well done! END OF SET E!

SET F
Test 1: Arithmetic

 10 MINS

Marks

1. 2 + 4 = [ ]

1

2. 13 − 6 = [ ]

1

3. 89 + 1 = [ ]

1

10 MINS

Marks

4. $5 + \boxed{} = 17$

1

5. $3 + 10 + 7 = \boxed{}$

1

6. $18 - 15 = \boxed{}$

1

Marks

1. Write the correct words to complete these sentences.

One more than eight is _____.

One less than thirteen is _____.

2

2. Match each shape to its name. One has been done for you.

| cube | cuboid | pyramid | sphere |

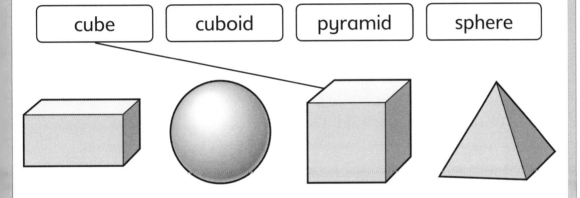

1

3. A fruit shop has 6 apples.

If 3 children share the apples equally between them, how many apples will they get each?

apples

1

10 MINS

4. Complete this snaking sum. The first two sums have been done for you.

Marks

	Start				
	2	+	3	=	5
					+
					1
					=
	☐	=	4	+	6
	+				
	☐				
	=				
	13	+	☐	=	15
				End	

1

Marks

5. John says:

> We do not have 10 fingers.
> We each have 8 fingers and
> 2 thumbs.

Using John's idea, say how many fingers and how many thumbs a group of 3 children have altogether.

 Show your working

| fingers | thumbs |

2

6. This shows which meal Class 1 has each day. Number the meals from 1 to 4 to show the order in which the class have them. The first one has been done for you.

Marks

Tomorrow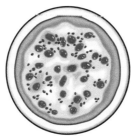

Today

Yesterday

1

Next week

1

Marks

1. 4 + 4 =

1

2. 17 − 0 =

1

3. 12 − 7 =

1

10 MINS

4. $98 + 3 =$ ☐

Marks

1

5. ☐ $- 13 = 4$

1

6. $9 + 12 =$ ☐

1

10 MINS

Marks

1. Circle the **two** numbers that are odd.

18   13

       14   7

1

2. Complete this table using numbers and words.

Numbers	Words
6	six
11	
	fifteen
20	

1

3. Tick the shape that has exactly $\frac{1}{4}$ shaded in blue.

A   **B**   **C**   **D**

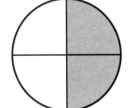

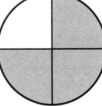

1

4. Look at these words.

| day |

| month |

| week |

| year |

a. Use **two** of these words to fill in the gaps below.

There are 12 months in a _____.

There are 7 days in a _____.

Marks

1

Look at these words.

| Sunday | | Tuesday | | Friday | | Thursday |

| Monday | | Saturday | | Wednesday |

b. Use **two** of these words to fill in the gaps below.

The day before Saturday is _____.

The day after Monday is _____.

1

KEEP IT
GOING!

10 MINS

5. Ahmed and Tim have been saving.

Ahmed has £12

Tim has £9

a. How much more money does Ahmed have than Tim?

£ ⬜

Marks

1

b. How much money do they have altogether?

£ ⬜

1

Well done! END OF SET G!

Marks

1. $8 - 8 = \boxed{}$

1

2. $33 - 1 = \boxed{}$

1

3. $3 + 4 + 5 = \boxed{}$

1

10 MINS

Marks

4. $7 + 7 = \boxed{}$

1

5. $16 - 10 = \boxed{}$

1

6. $14 + \boxed{} = 21$

1

10 MINS

Marks

1. What turn must the arrow make to point to 12?

Tick **one**.

A quarter turn

A half turn

A three-quarter turn

1

2. Look at these numbers.

Write each number **once** to make these number bonds correct.

8		7		6

$12 = 6 + \boxed{}$

$12 = 19 - \boxed{}$

$12 = \boxed{} + 4$

KEEP IT GOING!

1

44

10 MINS

3. Edward has a collection of toy figures.

Marks

A   B   C   D   E

a. How much taller is figure B than figure A?

Use a ruler.

cm

1

b. Write the letters for each figure in order, from shortest to tallest.

shortest   **tallest**

1

Marks

4. This is part of a 100 square.

Write the missing numbers to make it correct.

4	5	6	7	8
14	15		17	18
24				28
34				

1

5. Look at these signs.

+ − =

Write the missing sign to make these number sentences correct. One has been done for you.

3 + 2 = 5

3 ☐ 2 ☐ 1

5 ☐ 3 ☐ 2

5 ☐ 3 ☐ 8

1

6. A vet weighs some animals.

Marks

a. How much heavier is the dog than the cat?

kg

1

b. How much lighter is the guinea pig than the cat?

kg

1

Well done! END OF SET H!

SET 1
Test 1: Arithmetic

10 MINS

Marks

1. $3 + 3 = \boxed{}$

1

2. $\boxed{} - 4 = 6$

1

3. $12 - 5 = \boxed{}$

1

10 MINS

Marks

18 + 3 = ☐

1

5. 16 − ☐ = 2

1

6. 5 + 5 + 5 + 10 = ☐

1

Marks

1. A bus has 76 seats.

There is one spare seat.

How many people are sitting on the bus?

| people |

1

---

2. Match each number to its word. One has been done for you.

| 1 | 2 | 3 | 4 | 5 |

| two | one | five | three | four |

1

KEEP IT GOING!

Marks

3. Write the names of the **two** shapes used in this pattern.

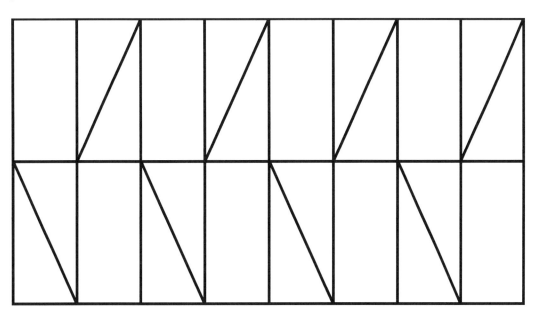

1. _____

2. _____

1

4. Circle the **shortest** time.

      50 minutes   10 minutes

         1 hour   70 minutes

1

Marks

5. Ed weighs 30kg.

His baby sister is **half** his weight.

a. What does Ed's sister weigh?

| kg |

1

His dad is **double** his weight.

b. What does Ed's dad weigh?

| kg |

1

Well done! END OF SET 1!

Answers
Maths

Q	Mark scheme for Set A Test 1 – Arithmetic	Marks
1	7	1
2	0	1
3	30	1
4	5	1
5	14	1
6	25	1
	Total	**6**

Q	Mark scheme for Set A Test 2 – Reasoning	Marks
1	18 **is more than** 15	1
2	OR	1
3	**a.** The boat is at the <u>bottom</u>. **b.** The ball is <u>below</u> the teddy.	1 1
4	13 counters	1
5	21p	1
	Total	**6**

Q	Mark scheme for Set B Test 1 – Arithmetic	Marks
1	6	1
2	15	1
3	10	1
4	57	1
5	3	1
6	31	1
	Total	**6**

Q	Mark scheme for Set B Test 2 – Reasoning	Marks
1	40 crayons	1
2	Accept 6 + 7 = 13; 7 + 6 = 13; 13 = 7 + 6; or 13 = 6 + 7	1
3	**Award 1 mark** for: cube, pyramid, sphere	1
4	The <u>pen</u> is the longest object.	1
5	20 wheels **Award 1 mark** for a correct method but with one arithmetical error.	2
6	11 marbles	1
	Total	7

Q	Mark scheme for Set C Test 1 – Arithmetic	Marks
1	4	1
2	13	1
3	2	1
4	18	1
5	99	1
6	19	1
	Total	6

Q	Mark scheme for Set C Test 2 – Reasoning	Marks
1		1
2	20 cups **Award 1 mark** for a correct method but with one arithmetical error.	2
3	Clock hands should show 7 o'clock. Hands should be accurate to within 2mm to award mark.	1
4	six, seven, <u>eight</u>, <u>nine</u>, ten	1
5	<u>C</u>, <u>A</u>, <u>B</u>	1
	Total	6

Q	Mark scheme for Set D Test 1 – Arithmetic	Marks
1	9	1
2	5	1
3	10	1
4	7	1
5	22	1
6	18	1
	Total	6

Q	Mark scheme for Set D Test 2 – Reasoning	Marks
1	square, triangle, circle	1
2	**9 + 7 = 15** is incorrect	1
3	5cm	1
4	7 strawberries	1
5	11 birds **Award 1 mark** if the correct approach to solving the problem is shown, but with a maximum of one arithmetical error.	2
6	Accept '3 fewer' or '3 less'.	1
	Total	**7**

Q	Mark scheme for Set E Test 1 – Arithmetic	Marks
1	2	1
2	11	1
3	15	1
4	9	1
5	20	1
6	5	1
	Total	**6**

Q	Mark scheme for Set E Test 2 – Reasoning	Marks
1	118cm	1
2	103	1
3	**a.** Various answers are possible, such as: The orange is heavier than the apple/pear/banana. OR The apple is heavier than the pear/banana. OR The pear is heavier than the banana. and The banana is lighter than the pear/apple/orange. OR The pear is lighter than the apple/orange. OR The apple is lighter than the orange. Check both answers are correct to award mark. **b.** orange and pear	1 1
4	90p **Award 1 mark** if the correct approach to solving the problem is shown, but with a maximum of one arithmetical error.	2
	Total	**6**

Q	Mark scheme for Set F Test 1 – Arithmetic	Marks
1	6	1
2	7	1
3	90	1
4	12	1
5	20	1
6	3	1
	Total	**6**

Q	Mark scheme for Set F Test 2 – Reasoning	Marks
1	One more than eight is <u>nine</u>. One less than thirteen is <u>twelve</u>. **Award 1 mark** for one correct answer.	2
2	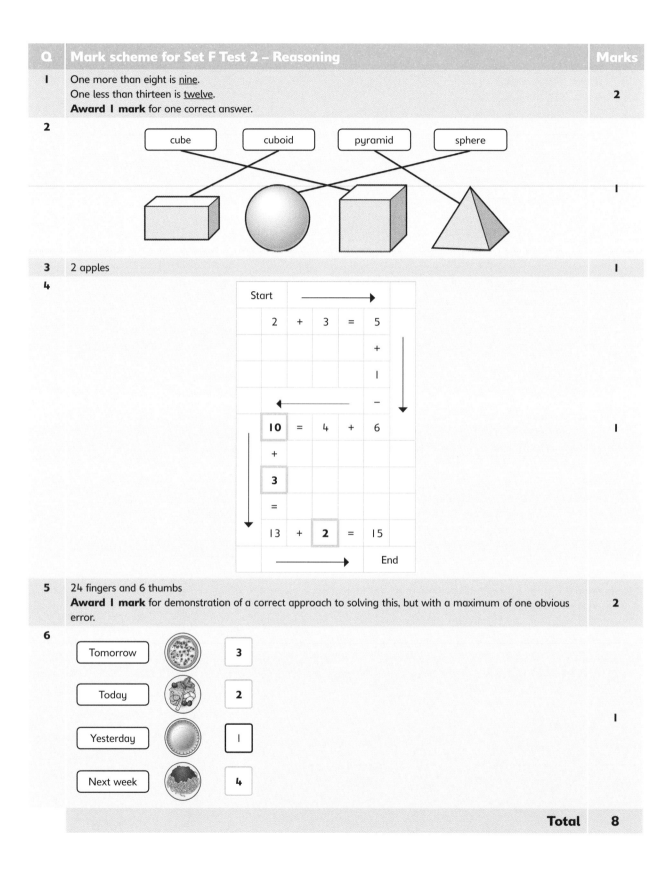	1
3	2 apples	1
4		1
5	24 fingers and 6 thumbs **Award 1 mark** for demonstration of a correct approach to solving this, but with a maximum of one obvious error.	2
6		1
	Total	8

56

Q	Mark scheme for Set G Test 1 – Arithmetic	Marks
1	8	1
2	17	1
3	5	1
4	101	1
5	17	1
6	21	1
	Total	**6**

Q	Mark scheme for Set G Test 2 – Reasoning	Marks
1	7, 13	1
2	<table><tr><td>6</td><td>six</td></tr><tr><td>11</td><td>eleven</td></tr><tr><td>15</td><td>fifteen</td></tr><tr><td>20</td><td>twenty</td></tr></table>	1
3	B	1
4	**a.** There are 12 months in a <u>year</u>. There are 7 days in a <u>week</u>.	1
	b. The day before Saturday is <u>Friday</u>. The day after Monday is <u>Tuesday</u>.	1
5	£3 £21	1 1
	Total	**7**

Q	Mark scheme for Set H Test 1 – Arithmetic	Marks
1	0	1
2	32	1
3	12	1
4	14	1
5	6	1
6	7	1
	Total	**6**

Q	Mark scheme for Set H Test 2 – Reasoning	Marks
1	A half turn	1
2	$12 = 6 +$ **6** $12 = 19 -$ **7** $12 =$ **8** $+ 4$	1
3	**a.** 4cm **b.** A, C, E, D, B	1 1
4	<table><tr><td>4</td><td>5</td><td>6</td><td>7</td><td>8</td></tr><tr><td>14</td><td>15</td><td>**16**</td><td>17</td><td>18</td></tr><tr><td>24</td><td>**25**</td><td>**26**</td><td>**27**</td><td>28</td></tr><tr><td>34</td><td>**35**</td><td>**36**</td><td>**37**</td><td>**38**</td></tr></table>	1
5	3 **+** 2 **=** 5 3 **–** 2 **=** 1 5 **–** 3 **=** 2 5 **+** 3 **=** 8 Note that there are other possibilities if the equals sign is inserted first, such as: $3 = 2 + 1$ OR $5 = 3 + 2$	1
6	**a.** 7kg **b.** 4kg	1 1
	Total	**8**

Q	Mark Scheme for Set I Test 1 – Arithmetic	Marks
1	6	1
2	10	1
3	7	1
4	21	1
5	14	1
6	25	1
	Total	**6**

Q	Mark Scheme for Set I Test 2 – Reasoning	Marks
1	75 people	1
2	**1** ✕ **2** **3** ✕ **4** ✕ **5** two one five three four	1
3	**1.** triangle **2.** rectangle	1
4	10 minutes	1
5	**a.** 15kg **b.** 60kg	1 1
	Total	**6**

General notes for parents and teachers:

The emphasis in the mathematics curriculum is on number, both as straight arithmetic as well as knowledge and reasoning.

Where a statement below indicates that the skill should be completed mentally, rough jottings are acceptable.

Number – number and place value

I can count to and across 100, forwards and backwards, beginning with 0 or 1, or from any given number, for example 98, 99, 100, 101, 102...

I can count, read and write numbers to 100 in numerals; and count in multiples of twos, fives and tens, for example 0, 5, 10, 15, 20...

I can, given a number, identify one more and one less, for example 1 less than 12 is 11.

I can identify and represent numbers using objects and pictorial representations including the number line, and use the language of: equal to, more than, less than (fewer), most and least, for example 12 is more than 10, but is less than 15.

I can read and write numbers from 1 to 20 in numerals and words, for example 16 is *sixteen*.

Number – addition and subtraction

I can read, write and interpret mathematical statements involving addition (+), subtraction (−) and equals (=) signs, for example $6 + 3 = 9$.

I can represent and use number bonds and related subtraction facts within 20, for example $14 + 6 = 20$; $20 − 14 = 6$.

I can add and subtract one-digit and two-digit numbers to 20, including zero, for example $13 − 7 = 6$.

I can solve one-step problems that involve addition and subtraction, using concrete objects and pictorial representations, and missing number problems, for example $7 = \boxed{} − 9$.

Number – multiplication and division

I can solve one-step problems involving multiplication and division, by calculating the answer using concrete objects, pictorial representations and arrays with the support of the teacher, for example 6 pens shared between 2 people gives 3 pens each.

Number – fractions

I can recognise, find and name a half as one of two equal parts of an object, shape or quantity, for example $\frac{1}{2}$ of 8 counters is 4 counters.

I can recognise, find and name a quarter as one of four equal parts of an object, shape or quantity, for example $\frac{1}{4}$ of 8 counters is 2 counters.

Measurement

I can compare, describe and solve practical problems for:
- lengths and heights, for example long/short, longer/shorter, tall/short, double/half.
- mass/weight, for example heavy/light, heavier than/lighter than.
- capacity and volume, for example full/empty, more than/less than, half, half full, quarter.
- time, for example quicker, slower, earlier, later.

I can measure and begin to record the following:
- lengths and heights, for example the box is 12cm high.
- mass/weight, for example the red teddy is lighter than the blue teddy.
- capacity and volume, for example the small cup holds 100ml of water.
- time, for example three o'clock is later than two o'clock.

I can recognise and know the value of different denominations of coins and notes, for example there is 25p on the table.

I can sequence events in chronological order using language, for example before and after, next, first, today, yesterday, tomorrow, morning, afternoon and evening.

I can recognise and use language relating to dates, including days of the week, weeks, months and years, for example *Her birthday is in December. This year it is on a Thursday.*

I can tell the time to the hour and half past the hour and draw the hands on a clock face to show these times, for example the clock says half-past five.

I can recognise and name common 2D and 3D shapes, including:

- 2D shapes, for example rectangles (including squares), circles and triangles.
- 3D shapes, for example cuboids (including cubes), pyramids and spheres.

I can describe position, direction and movement, including whole, half, quarter and three-quarter turns, for example *The robot has done a half turn.*

Progress chart

Fill in your score in the table below to see how well you've done.

	Score
SET A	
SET B	
SET C	
SET D	
SET E	
SET F	
SET G	
SET H	
SET I	
TOTAL	

Mark	
0–50	Good try! You need more practice in some topics – ask an adult to help you.
51–75	You're doing really well. Ask for extra help for any topics you found tricky.
76–115	You're a 10-Minute SATS Test maths star – good work!

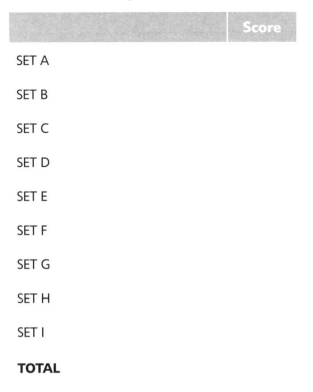

GREAT WORK!

Well done!

You have completed all of the 10-Minute SATs Tests

Name: _____

Date: _____

SCHOLASTIC

Prepare for SATs Success

BOOSTER
Tests & Workbooks

Give SATs results an extra boost

978-1407-16853-1

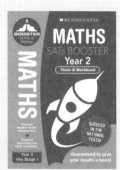

978-1407-16858-6

978-1407-16848-7

978-1407-16085-6

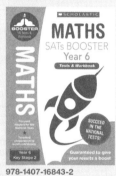

978-1407-16843-2

978-1407-16081-8

CHALLENGE
Workbooks & Skills Tests

For children looking for extra stretch

978-1407-17649-9

978-1407-17543-0

978-1407-17553-9

978-1407-17654-3

978-1407-17548-5

978-1407-17558-4

Find out more at www.scholastic.co.uk/assessment

QUICK TESTS FOR SATs SUCCESS

BOOST YOUR CHILD'S CONFIDENCE WITH 10-MINUTE SATs TESTS

- Bite-size mini SATs tests which take just 10 minutes to complete

- Covers key National Test topics

- Full answers and progress chart provided to track improvement

- Available for Years 1 to 6

Find out more at www.scholastic.co.uk